TOP HIGH SCHOOL SPORTS
SOCCER

A Crabtree Branches Book

THOMAS KINGSLEY TROUPE

CRABTREE
Publishing Company
www.crabtreebooks.com

School-to-Home Support for Caregivers and Teachers

This high-interest book is designed to motivate striving students with engaging topics while building fluency, vocabulary, and an interest in reading. Here are a few questions and activities to help the reader build upon his or her comprehension skills.

Before Reading:
- What do I think this book is about?
- What do I know about this topic?
- What do I want to learn about this topic?
- Why am I reading this book?

During Reading:
- I wonder why...
- I'm curious to know...
- How is this like something I already know?
- What have I learned so far?

After Reading:
- What was the author trying to teach me?
- What are some details?
- How did the photographs and captions help me understand more?
- Read the book again and look for the vocabulary words.
- What questions do I still have?

Extension Activities:
- What was your favorite part of the book? Write a paragraph on it.
- Draw a picture of your favorite thing you learned from the book.

TABLE OF CONTENTS

GOOOOOOOAL!!! 4
Soccer History 6
Soccer Season 8
High School Soccer Teams 10
Basics of the Game 12
Offense 14
Defense 16
Midfielders 18
Equipment and Uniforms 20
Practice and Training 22
Soccer Jargon 24
Playoffs and State Tournaments 26
Conclusion 28
Glossary 30
Index 31
Websites to Visit 31
About the Author 32

GOOOOOOOAL!!!

The ball is booted your way. You take the ball and drive to the goal as a defender quickly approaches. You dribble and turn, faking your opponent out. You wind up, kick, and the ball soars toward the net. The goalie never saw it coming! GOAL!

Jump into your cleats and get in a good stretch. We're about to learn why soccer ranks among the...TOP HIGH SCHOOL SPORTS.

FUN FACT

Soccer is the most popular sport in the world, with an estimated following of four billion fans.

SOCCER HISTORY

Soccer is easily one of the oldest sports that is still played today. Its origins date as far back as 206 B.C. where Chinese soldiers played Tsu'chu, which means "kicking the ball." It was the first game to not allow hands.

In Europe and most of the rest of the world, soccer is called football. In the United States and Canada, the term football refers to gridiron football, as played in the National Football League (NFL). Over time, people in the two countries started using the term soccer to make it less confusing between the two sports.

Soccer balls from earlier times.

SOCCER SEASON

For most high schools, the soccer season begins in fall and is played until the beginning of winter. Some high schools have multiple soccer seasons that include fall, winter, and spring.

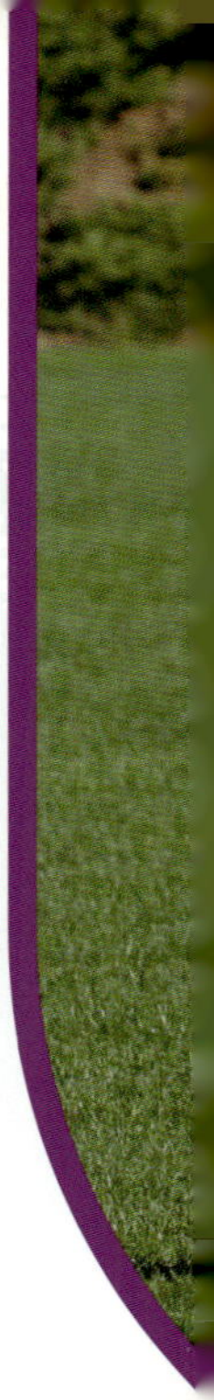

A typical high school game is two 40-minute periods or four 20-minute quarters with a 10-minute overtime. Most schools will have a team for boys and a separate team for girls. Others play **co-ed** soccer.

> ### FUN FACT
> During the Middle Ages in Europe (500–1500 CE), soccer balls were made from inflated pig bladders. Gross! In 1855, Charles Goodyear designed the first vulcanized rubber soccer ball. With a consistent shape, the ball was much easier to kick around and control.

HIGH SCHOOL SOCCER TEAMS

High schools usually form at least two soccer teams, depending on school size and interest. The varsity teams are where the third- and fourth-year students typically play. The school's strongest athletes compete at the varsity level.

Junior varsity teams are made up of first- and second-year students. At this level, they improve their skills to be able to try out for the varsity team in third or fourth year.

A size 5 adult soccer ball is used during high school soccer games. It has a diameter of 8.6–9 inches (22–23 cm) and a circumference of 27–28 inches (69–71 cm). There are usually three balls available to use during a game in case a ball is lost or damaged.

BASICS OF THE GAME

The basics of soccer are **straightforward**. Two teams of 11 compete on a large field with goals on each end. Players move the ball across the field with their feet and kick the ball into the net to score.

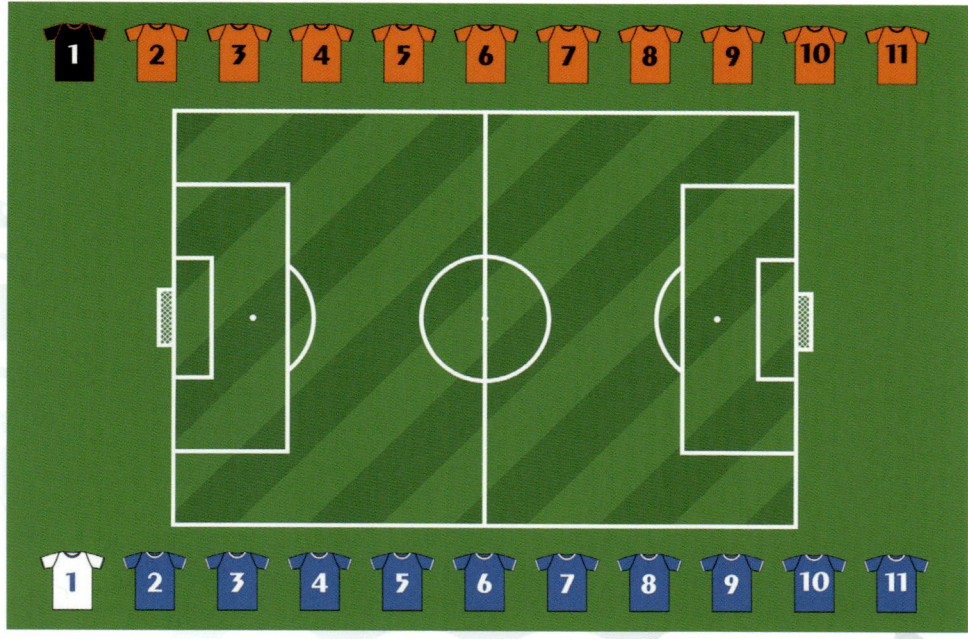

Each goal is worth one point. A violation of the rules may result in a **penalty** kick, giving a player a free shot at the goal. Referees monitor the field during games to make sure the rules are followed!

> High school soccer fields can range from a number of different sizes. They are anywhere between 55 to 80 yards (50–73 m) wide and 100 to 120 yards (91–110 m) long. In the U.S., the standard is set by the National Federation of State High School Associations (NFHS).

OFFENSE

There are 11 players from each team out on the field at once. Here is what the **offensive** squad looks like:

Left Striker — Positioned to the left side of the other team's goal, this player's job is to score. They will be swarmed by defenders, trying to stop that from happening.

Center Forward — The center moves the ball into opponent territory. This player sets up kicks to the goal and tries to score themselves.

Right Striker — Positioned on the right side of the goal, this player's job is also to stay close for goal opportunities. Fast players who can **outmaneuver** defenders play as strikers.

CENTER FORWARD

STRIKER

Offensive players are usually the quickest team members on a soccer team. It's necessary for them to be able to make a shot from many angles. They also have to ensure that they don't get called offside.

DEFENSE

Because soccer is played around the world, there can be different names for each position. Below are the common names for the defensive crew:

Sweeper — Positioned between the goalie and defensive line, the sweeper's job is to "sweep up" any balls that get past the main **defense**.

Left & Right Defenders
(also known as fullbacks or wingbacks) — Defenders on the left and right sides of the field whose job is to protect their side and center-back when needed.

Center-back
(Central Defender, Center Fullback, Stopper) — The center-back plays in the middle of the rear defensive line and can hang back to defend the goal.

LEFT FULL-BACK

MIDFIELDERS

The midfielders play exactly where one would expect: in the middle of the field. They work as the link that connects the offense and defensive teams.

Left & Right Midfielders (Wingers, Outside Midfielders) — These players are positioned wide, to keep the other team's offense from running down the middle. Their job is to make sure to keep the ball back in offensive play.

Center Midfielder — This is one of the hardest positions on the team. This player can play both defensively or offensively, depending on where the ball is moving. A good center midfielder has top level ball-handling skills.

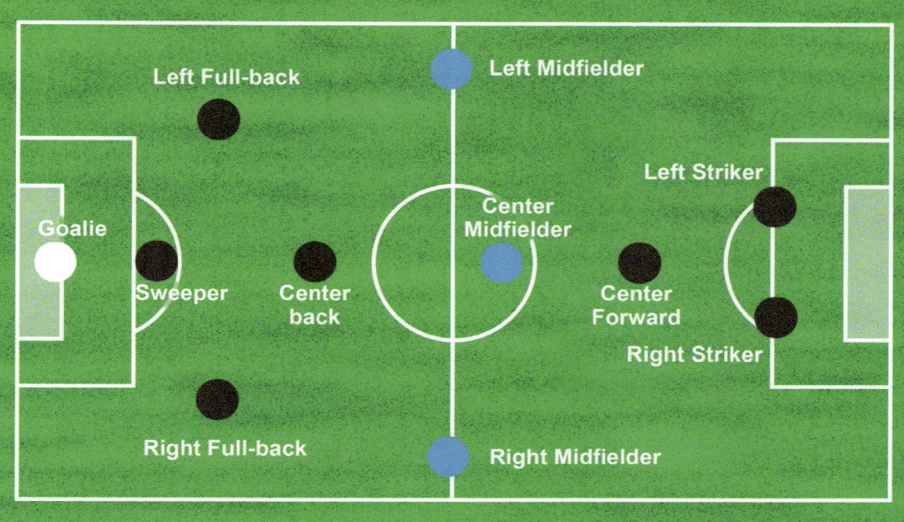

CENTER MIDFIELDER

FUN FACT

In Europe, a soccer field is sometimes referred to as a "pitch." This name dates back to the 1200s in England.

EQUIPMENT AND UNIFORMS

Soccer is a fast-moving sport where players are running constantly. To keep cool, they usually wear short sleeved jerseys, shorts, and long socks. Cleats are worn to help grip the turf and keep players from slipping.

Cleats

For protection from kicking legs and feet, shin-guards are worn. Mouth guards protect their teeth.

FUN FACT

The numbers on soccer jerseys aren't random. They are usually assigned depending on the player's position on the field. For example, the goalie is usually 1, defensive players are 2-5 and so on!

A custom-fitted mouth guard.

PRACTICE AND TRAINING

Soccer practice is held after school and lasts usually 60-90 minutes. Because soccer is a sport that can be played year round, practice space might be outdoors or in an indoor soccer arena.

During practice, players will work on ball-handling, passing, and shooting drills. Since the majority of the game is running, players should expect to do a lot of sprinting to keep their **stamina** up!

SOCCER JARGON

Just like a lot of sports, soccer has many interesting phrases that might confuse newer players.

Here are some of the most common ones:

- **Assist** — when a player passes the ball to another player, who scores the goal.
- **Bicycle Kick** — a backwards somersault kick that launches the ball in the opposite direction.
- **Dribble** — moving and controlling the ball down the field with your feet.
- **Dummy** — faking that the ball is coming to you to trick an opponent.
- **Head** — to hit the ball with the forehead.
- **Spot-kick** — a penalty kick, placed 12 yards in front of the goal.
- **Tackle** — to steal the ball from another player with your own feet.

DRIBBLE

HEAD

SPOT-KICK

PLAYOFFS AND STATE TOURNAMENTS

High school soccer teams usually compete with other schools to see which team is the best. Schools can participate in state playoffs and state championship **tournaments**.

Like many schools, teams are broken into classes depending on the number of students enrolled in the high school. Large schools face off against larger schools and smaller schools compete against small schools. This allows for fair competition!

FUN FACT

In 2019 over 459,000 boys and over 394,000 girls in the United States competed in a high school soccer program!

CONCLUSION

Soccer is one of the most fast-paced and competitive sports high-schoolers participate in. Players will need speed, endurance, and skill to keep their team winning. The sweat and hard work is worth it!

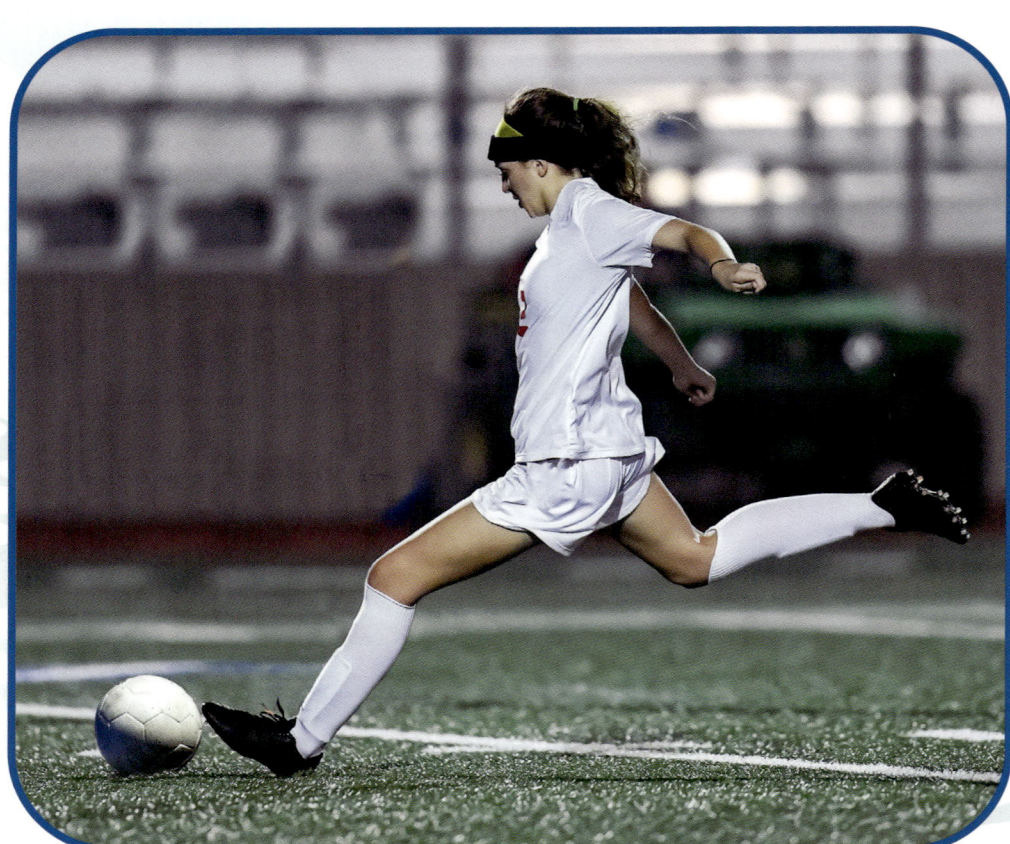

Will you show off your moves on the soccer field? You and your team could come out on top at a major tournament. With a winning attitude and some fancy footwork, you'll see why soccer is easily one of the TOP HIGH SCHOOL SPORTS!

GLOSSARY

co-ed (KOH-ed): something that includes both male and females

defense (DEE-fenss): defending a goal against the opposing team

offensive (AW-fenss-iv): the team possessing the ball in an attempt to score

outmaneuver (OUT-muhn-oo-vur): evading an opponent with speed and agility

penalty (PEN-uhl-tee): a punishment for breaking a rule

stamina (STAM-in-uh): ability to keep moving for longer periods of time

straightfoward (strayt-FOR-wurd): uncomplicated and easy to understand

tournaments (TOR-nuh-muhntz): a series of contests or games played between competing teams

vulcanized (VOL-kuhn-ized): rubber heated with sulfur to make it easier to shape

INDEX

cleats 5, 20
defense 16
footwork 29
Goodyear, Charles 9
midfielders 18

offense 14, 18
stamina 23
striker 14, 15
varsity 10, 11

WEBSITES TO VISIT

https://www.ducksters.com/sports/soccer.php

https://www.dkfindout.com/us/sports/soccer/

https://www.sportsrec.com/5093685/facts-about-soccer-for-kids

ABOUT THE AUTHOR

Thomas Kingsley Troupe

Thomas Kingsley Troupe is the author of a big ol' pile of books for kids. He's written about everything from ghosts to Bigfoot to third grade werewolves. He even wrote a book about dirt. When he's not writing or reading, he gets plenty of exercise and remembers sacking quarterbacks while on his high school football team. Thomas lives in Woodbury, Minnesota with his two sons.

Written by: Thomas Kingsley Troupe
Designed by: Jennifer Dudyk
Edited by: Kelli Hicks
Proofreader: Ellen Rodger

Photographs: Following images from Shutterstock.com: Cover background pattern (and pattern throughout book © HNK, soccer ball on cover and title page Pasko Maksim, cover photo of male players © JoeSAPhotos, cover photo of female players © Monkey Business Images. Page 4 © Monkey Business Images, Page 5 top image © matimix, Page 7 bottom photo © verzellenberg, Page 8 top photo © Patsy Michaud, Page 9 © Larry St. Pierre, Page 10 top photo © Monkey Business Images, Page 10 bottom photo and Page 11 top photo © JustPixs, Page 13 © BRG.photography, Page 14, 17, and 19 diagram © hermanthos, Page 15 top photo © JoeSAPhotos, bottom photo © Larry St. Pierre, Page 21 illustration © Nattanopdesign, photo © baklykovadaria, Page 22 g matimix, Page 23 bottom photo © WoodysPhotos, Page 24 and Page 25 both top photos © JoeSAPhotos, Page 25 bottom photo © koonsiri boonnak, Page 26 top photo © JustPixs, bottom photo © matimix, Page 27 © Elkhophoto, Page 28 © JoeSAPhotos, Page 29 top photo © sirtravelalot, bottom photo © Larry St. Pierre. Following images from istock by Getty Images: Page 5 bottom photo © Ohmega1982, Page 8 bottom photo © KuntalSaha, Page 11 soccer ball © vlastas, Page 20 top photo and Page 23 top photo © matimix, bottom photo © venakr. Following images from Dreamstime.com: Page 12 photo © David Wood, diagram © Alberto Ragnoli, Page 17 photo © Thomas Carter, Page 19 photo © Robert Philip. Black and white photos Pages 6 and 7 photo courtesy of the Library of Congress.

Library and Archives Canada Cataloguing in Publication

CIP available at Library and Archives Canada

Library of Congress Cataloging-in-Publication Data

CIP available at Library of Congress

Crabtree Publishing Company
www.crabtreebooks.com   1-800-387-7650

Printed in the U.S.A./CG20210915/012022

Copyright © 2022 **CRABTREE PUBLISHING COMPANY**

All rights reserved. No part of this publication may be reproduced, stored in a retrieval system or be transmitted in any form or by any means, electronic, mechanical, photocopying, recording, or otherwise, without the prior written permission of Crabtree Publishing Company. In Canada: We acknowledge the financial support of the Government of Canada through the Canada Book Fund for our publishing activities.

Published in the United States
Crabtree Publishing
347 Fifth Avenue, Suite 1402-145
New York, NY, 10016

Published in Canada
Crabtree Publishing
616 Welland Ave.
St. Catharines, Ontario L2M 5V6